LONDON COUNTRY BUSES
A Colour Portfolio

Michael H. C. Baker

Foreword

The London bus scene has changed dramatically over the last 30 years, none more so than the former Country Area of London Transport's operations.

January 1970 saw the formation of a new company, London Country Bus Services Ltd, and the start of a series of events that would transform virtually everything that had preceded it: the disappearance of crew operation, the closure and demolition of all but a handful of the inherited garages and the removal or replacement of vast volumes of familiar bus related roadside furniture. The practice of leasing vehicles was adopted and vehicle types came and went almost as frequently as the service timetables. The prewar Green Line coach network was abandoned in favour of commuter routes and excursions. The list is endless, but for those who have witnessed it, the transition has been interesting if tinged with regret.

For some, the calling of those increasingly revered distant days is all too strong and preservation of all kinds of associated artifacts comforts the loss. It is therefore with gratitude that a percentage of the sales from this book will be donated to the rebuild of STL2377 which although not a country bus itself, is identical to those that were.

Peter Plummer
Chair, London Bus Preservation Trust
February 2000

Title page: MBA292 heads through St Albans on local route S3 in March 1977. Whilst the MBAs were really Swifts, London Transport and London Country always called them Merlins, leaving the (later) SM family as Swifts. The first AEC Merlin entered service on an experimental basis with London Transport in April 1966 and eventually 665 were operated in red and green liveries. They were, by any measurement, the least successful design to work either in the Central or Country areas. If Oscars were given for monumentally bad buses, the Merlins would have walked away unchallenged. They were unreliable in just about every respect: chassis, engine and bodywork caused numerous problems. All the London Country ones had been withdrawn by 1980, London Transport's last ones being taken out of passenger service in April 1981. *Geoff Rixon*

First published 2000

ISBN 0 7110 2730 7

Published by Ian Allan Publishing

an imprint of Ian Allan Publishing Ltd, Terminal House, Shepperton, Surrey TW17 8AS.
Printed by Ian Allan Printing Ltd, Riverdene Business Park, Hersham, Surrey KT12 4RG.

Code: 0008/B2

Introduction

It was on 1 January 1970 that London Country Bus Services was created as a subsidiary of the National Bus Company. As a result of the Transport (London) Act of 1969, the Country Bus & Coach Department of London Transport was transferred to the newly-created NBC. London Country inherited both the Country (green) buses as well as Green Line, resulting in continued operation into central London. In theory, a change of ownership should have led to dramatic differences; in reality, at least for the initial period, London Country retained much that was common with London Transport. The livery changed subtly and the traditional London bus types were gradually withdrawn or replaced as new types appeared, but the major changes were only really to occur towards the end of the London Country era, as the company was split up as a prelude to privatisation and deregulation.

Although 1970 did not mark a seismic shift to the casual viewer, it did represent a considerable alteration to the structure of bus operation within the southeast of England. The Country Area owed much of its existence to the gradual expansion of the London General Omnibus Company in the period prior to the setting up of the London Passenger Transport Board in 1933. The creation of London Country meant that, for the first time in several generations, there was no common ownership between the Central and Country areas. The National Bus Company

Below left: STL 2417 in service at Godstone garage in 1940. *D. W. K. Jones*

Right: The GS-type represented the postwar successor of the prewar Leyland Cubs. A total of 84 entered service from 1953. Being a nationalised company, London Transport was entitled to buy ECW body-work and thus these modified Guy Vixens were fitted with 26-seat bodywork which was instantly recognisable as being of ECW design, although there were LT touches too. GS5 is seen in the bus station at Hertford on 16 September 1961. *Hugh Ramsey*

acquired a subsidiary that was financially suspect — it had lost more than half a million pounds in both of the previous years — and was facing the reality of operation in an environment where car ownership and increasing prosperity made many of its services ever more marginal.

During the 1970s London Country attempted to improve its position through redefining its services in many of its most important urban centres — such as Stevenage and Crawley — and by the gradual reduction of its more financially demanding services. Through its vehicle replacement policy, many of the traditional London Transport designs that it inherited — such as the Routemasters, and some RTs — were sold back to London Transport, to be replaced by increasing numbers of vehicles suitable for one-person operation. Other traditional types — such

as the RT and RF — were to disappear from London Country service as obsolescent during the late 1970s. In order to replace these vehicles, London Country acquired a motley collection of types; some of these were new, others were distinctly elderly. A common theme through much of the decade was the appearance of second-hand or borrowed vehicles from a remarkable selection of other operators, including Eastbourne and Bournemouth corporations and fellow NBC subsidiaries Ribble and Southdown.

Some 30 years after the creation of London Country, we are fortunate that there were individuals who travelled round the region recording in colour the changing Country Area scene. In this second volume devoted to London Country and its predecessor, we turn the clock back to the 1960s and 1970s to

Left: London Transport's standard postwar single-deck type was the RF AEC Regal IV with Metro-Cammell bodywork. A total of 700 was delivered between 1951 and 1953. They were used on all manner of duties and were extremely long-lived. RF59 of Stevenage garage was originally a Green Line coach but is seen here converted to 38-seat bus format for use in the Country Area. The picture dates from June 1973. *Geoff Rixon*

Right: XF8 stands gleaming in the sun at Stevenage garage on 6 September 1971. Eight of these standard provincial Park Royal-bodied H41/31F Daimler Fleetlines were bought by London Transport for evaluation in the Country Area in 1965. One of London Transport's last acts was to repaint three XFs at the end of 1969 in this striking livery for the Stevenage Blue Arrow commuter service. London Country later repainted them green and they ended their days with the rest of their class working out of East Grinstead garage. *R. C. Riley*

recall the two decades that straddle the creation of London Country.

The intention with this book is not to provide a detailed history of London Country and its operations during the 1960s and 1970s. Rather it is hoped that the content will act as a reminder for all those who recall the nature of the bus industry in the period before deregulation and privatisation wrought dramatic changes.

The success of the first volume of London Country was pleasing for it is perhaps inevitable that when we think of the London bus we think of red double-deck vehicles. Indeed, all sorts of less-than-authentic specimens can be found masquerading as such in tourist traps in various parts of the world. But if you were brought up, as I was, in the London

suburbs, then green-liveried Country Area buses and Green Line coaches were as integral a part of the great LT empire as their Central Area counterparts. Today, whilst red is still the colour of central London and inner suburban buses, operations in the former Country Area are now so diverse that it must be hard for the younger generation of enthusiasts to believe that they were ever unified and that buses identical in every respect could be found as far apart as Luton, Tilbury, Forest Row, Slough and Aylesbury.

Michael H. C. Baker
Wareham
March 2000

Above: Although it was in late 1969, at the very end of LT's ownership, that the first experiments in improved services for Stevenage commenced, it was under LCBS ownership that these developed into Superbus with vehicles painted in the striking blue and yellow livery. On 6 September 1971, AEC Swift SM497, one of a number repainted into Superbus livery, awaits departure with a service to Chells. *R. C. Riley*

Right: A total of 120 Leyland Atlanteans was delivered to London Country in 1972. Of these, the first 90 were ordered by London Country and the remaining 30 were originally destined for Midland Red. The former were bodied by Park Royal and the latter by Metro-Cammell-Weymann. One of the MCW-bodied examples, AN103, is seen at St Albans on 22 June 1976 in the somewhat ill-judged dark green and vivid yellow livery which was soon to be replaced by National leaf green, white and grey. National livery was in general a poor substitute for what had gone before, but in London Country's case many considered it was actually an improvement. Alongside the AN are two Merlins, MBS430 and MBS400. *R. C. Riley*

Left: On 22 June 1976 RT4792 heads towards Hatfield garage on route 341 in St Albans. *R. C. Riley*

Above: A year earlier, on 10 June 1975, RF141 is pictured standing outside St Albans garage in Green Line livery. By the mid-1970s, the 20-year-old RFs were starting to look their age as far as express services were concerned, although the type survived in Green Line service until the last years of the decade. *R. C. Riley*

Left: Out in the country south of Dunstable, RF265 heads towards the A5, followed by a Court Line Plaxton Panorama-bodied coach, on route 360, which ran from Luton to Dunstable via Caddington. The date is Saturday 9 September 1972. *Hugh Ramsey*

Above: The Square, Dunstable, is pictured on a sunny May morning in 1969. On the left is RF579 in original Country Area bus livery on the 342 route, alongside refurbished coach RF100 about to set off for Dorking — although the blind has not yet been wound on. By this date, working of the 713 north of St Albans was drawing to a close; services were terminated at St Albans (with the exception of peak hour services and Sundays) on 29 May 1971 and the route was to see further revisions in the mid-1970s until it was finally withdrawn (being replaced by a new service to Luton Airport) in early 1977. *Hugh Ramsey*

Left: Twelve Marshall-bodied AEC (note the badge) Swifts were delivered to South Wales Transport in 1971 and transferred when a few months old to London Country. One of these, SMW8, a 53-seat bus, is seen on the forecourt of Hatfield garage in February 1981 working out its final months with London Country. The vehicles spent the bulk of their career with London Country allocated to St Albans, where they replaced AEC Merlins. *Geoff Rixon*

Below: St Albans is viewed in May 1973 with the cathedral in the background and a pair of St Albans-based buses in the foreground. Bound for Regent's Park Zoo's rural outpost, Whipsnade, is long-lived RF85 of 1951, which had been demoted from Green Line status to bus work, alongside another Marshall-bodied AEC Swift, SMW6. The latter passed to the breakers in December 1981. There were 15 members of the SMW class; the original three, diverted from South Wales Transport in 1969, were bodied by Willowbrook. *Geoff Lumb*

Left: Looking absolutely immaculate is Country bus RF567 standing outside the front door of its residence at St Albans on Saturday 20 May 1968. *Hugh Ramsey*

Above: Brand-new Park Royal-bodied Leyland Atlantean AN65 stands in St Peter's Street, St Albans, on Saturday 9 September 1972 prior to heading south on the 321 route to Uxbridge. The 321 linked Luton with Uxbridge, running via Harpenden, St Albans, Watford and Rickmansworth. By this date the 321 service had lost much of its importance as a trunk route with the launch, in 1967, of the Green Line service from Luton to Crawley (the 727). *Hugh Ramsey*

15

Left: RT3752 was the last member of its class in passenger service north of the river. It is seen here, at Uxbridge, working from Garston garage, with a complete set of well-maintained blinds on 14 March 1977, a month before withdrawal.
Peter Plummer

Right: The first of four RTs to acquire National Bus Company livery was RT2367, which appeared thus in January 1975. It was confined to training duties from Hertford garage and is seen here at St Albans on 10 June 1975. *R. C. Riley*

CAUTION
DRIVER UNDER
INSTRUCTION

LONDON COUNTRY

RT 2367

L

KGU 396

Left: RT1018 was one of the three RTs which not only acquired NBC livery but were put into passenger service, from Chelsham garage. RT1018 was later transferred to training duties north of the river and is seen here, on 13 May 1978, occupying the same spot where RT2367 was recorded nearly three years earlier. *Geoff Rixon*

Above: Another provincial-type bus to serve with London Transport was the Willowbrook-bodied AEC Reliance. This experimental class of three entered service in September 1960 at Hemel Hempstead and did the rounds of various garages before being sold to Chesterfield Corporation in 1963. Two of the RW class, Nos 2 and 3, were preserved, RW2 being seen here at Catford garage on 7 June 1980. *R. C. Riley*

Below: In the early 1950s, the Country Area required a replacement for the Leyland Cubs used on lightly trafficked routes. The result was 26-seat Guy Special (GS) class. In total, 84 of the class were delivered in 1953/4. All 84 were fitted with Eastern Coach Works bodywork on the 14ft 9in wheelbase modified Guy Vixen chassis. The GS type was fitted with a derated Perkins P6 six-cylinder engine. Hemel Hempstead operated several members of the class. GS51 is seen here on its way to Chesham in around 1960. *Photobus/Alastair Douglas*

Right: Leyland National SNB505 heads through Chesham before venturing out into the snow-covered Chilterns on its way to High Wycombe in January 1982 on the 362 route. *Geoff Rixon*

RML2418 is captured working a High Wycombe town service on 23 August 1977. This bus was at the time allocated to High Wycombe (HE) garage. By this date, the London Country garage in High Wycombe — Queen Alexandra Road — was coming to the end of its operational life; all London Country services in the town were operated from Amersham garage from 1 October 1977. Services in the town were shared with Alder Valley, and local routes — including the 326 (which had traditionally been interlinked with Alder Valley's 26/26A services)— were altered from 13 April 1980 as a result of a Market Analysis Project exercise. *Peter Plummer*

RML2456, with a nearly full complement of no doubt satisfied customers, heads through the conifers of Denham on 6 May 1978. Although bearing a Staines (ST) allocation, the bus was actually based at Garston (GR). By September the 347A had gone over to one-person operation and RML2456 was delicensed. In July 1979 the bus was sold to London Transport and is now in the ownership of Stagecoach East London. It currently operates over route 15 out of Upton Park garage. *Geoff Rixon*

The RLH was essentially a Regent III — a provincial version of the RT — and the resemblance is obvious, although the 76 members of the class had Weymann bodies of four-bay design and slide vents rather than half-drop windows. Delivered between 1950 and 1953, the first 20 had been intended for Midland General. RLH27 seen here was of the second, 1952 batch, and is temporarily working from Harrow Weald garage on Central Area route 230. *Photobus/Roy Marshall*

A much earlier Regent, ST821, was delivered to National, one of the predecessors of London Transport's Country Area, in 1931. Virtually identical to its red brothers, it was withdrawn in 1949 and became the only one of its type to enter the London Transport collection. A friend told me that the Country Area ST was his favourite bus, not least because those in the Windsor area, where he lived, always featured a selection of dead flies that could be observed from the upstairs front seat bouncing around on the window sill. ST821 is seen here in Ash Grove garage at the end of 1998 about to head off to Covent Garden and, ultimately, its new home at Acton. Beyond is the preserved Green Line T219 of 1930. *Author*

25

Above: Eccleston Bridge, above Victoria station, was associated for decades with Green Line. Here RF551, a Country bus, is pressed into Green Line service on the 706 Chelsham-Aylesbury service in early 1970. The route disappeared in 1977, and in 1979 the 706 route number was reallocated to the Tunbridge Wells-Victoria service. *Geoff Lumb*

Right: A rather unexpected addition to the hugely varied panoply of vehicles which have operated London Transport's Central London sightseeing tour was London Country's AN116, an MCW-bodied Atlantean of 1972. It is seen here at Victoria on 17 September 1982. *R. C. Riley*

Left: The preserved T219, one of the standard front-entrance Duple-bodied coaches introduced in 1930/1 which ensured the success of the Green Line network. The supremely dignified livery suited the handsome lines of this AEC Regal, seen here on display at Covent Garden at the end of 1998. Replaced by the 10T10s, Qs and TFs in the late 1930s, most of these vehicles served as buses until the RF era. T219 was withdrawn in November 1950 and restored to its original 1930s Green Line condition. *Author*

Above: During their long careers, many green RFs were sometimes seen working red Central Area routes. RF577 is pictured in the heart of Central Area single-deck territory on loan to Kingston garage in about 1967. The vehicle is operating on the 219 route towards Weybridge station; this service was eventually to form part of an extended London Country route 437 to Guildford. *Photobus/Geoffrey Morant*

Above: Four Green Line vehicles line up at Windsor in the mid-1970s. The three single-deck vehicles are members of the 90-strong RP class of 45-seat Park Royal-bodied AEC Reliances, delivered between November 1971 and April 1972. Two of these, Nos 28 and 57, are in National suburban coach livery, whilst RP41, on the right, is in original Lincoln green. Downgraded to buses in the late 1970s, the RP type continued to appear as Green Line reliefs. RT3520, on the extreme right, is also acting as a Green Line relief. Another RT and an RF are in the second rank. *Geoff Rixon*

Right: A Reliance on bus duties: RP22, of Weybridge garage, heads down the Portsmouth Road in Thames Ditton on 31 January 1983 towards Guildford on the 437 service. The 437 originally linked Weybridge with Guildford; however, the service was extended from Weybridge to Kingston replacing the former LT service 219 illustrated earlier. At the time of this photograph, London Country operation was a recent innovation, having only commenced on 29 January 1983. *Geoff Rixon*

Left: RN3 heads southwest through Hampton Court on 7 December 1980. It may look like a coach and it may be working a Green Line route — although there is a suspicious and complete absence of passengers — but it was actually a 60-seat bus. New to Barton Transport in 1972, 10 of these Plaxton Panorama Elite-bodied AEC Reliances were seated with a three-plus-two layout, and no headrests, and bought by London Country in 1977. Although much used on school contracts, they often found themselves on Green Line work. It is a moot point whether they or Leyland Nationals were the most unsuitable for these duties. *Geoff Rixon*

Above: RLH21 heads for Guildford during the summer of 1969 on the 436, one of the routes that required lowbridge buses. Seventeen RLHs were taken into London Country ownership in January 1970, but all had been replaced by one-person single-deck buses by August of that year. *Photobus/Arnold Richardson*

Left: RT628 of Guildford garage works a local service in the town during April 1969. *Dave Brown*

Above: A varied Sunday line-up is seen at Leatherhead garage in September 1978. From left to right are BL52, a London Transport Bristol LH/ECW working a route which not much earlier had employed RTs; BN43, a London Country 35-seat LHS of 1974; Atlantean AN36; and RMC1475. *Roy Hobbs*

Above: RF79, a former Green Line vehicle, was withdrawn from bus duties in 1977 before being converted into a towing vehicle and repainted in this rather striking livery. It is seen at Leatherhead garage in June 1979. *Geoff Rixon*

Above right: On 26 July 1973, RF230 is pictured at Leatherhead whilst running on the 462. *R. C. Riley*

Right: One of the attractions of Derby Day at Epsom has always been the variety of vehicles used to transport punters to the racecourse. Here, in June 1981, RN9 of Dorking, with all 60 seats occupied, climbs the hill towards the Downs on route 406F. This route was one of two special services linked to the main 406; the other — 406C — carried printers to the Windmill Press at Kingswood. *Geoff Rixon*

Left: RT3461, one of the few RTs repainted into full NBC livery and allocated to Chelsham, takes time out from its usual duties on the 403 and 453 to transport race-goers from Epsom station to the racecourse for the Derby on 1 June 1977.
Peter Plummer

Right: A regular visitor to Epsom Downs was the 406 route. Out on its own, ahead of the field, RMC1464, of Leatherhead garage, rounds Tattenham Corner in March 1976. The 406 linked Kingston with Redhill, travelling via Surbiton, Tolworth, Epsom and Reigate. The origins of the route dated back to 5 June 1920 when the East Surrey Traction Co introduced a service between Redhill Market Place and Epsom. The route was extended to Kingston on 14 April 1922 and was allocated the route number 406 on 1 December 1924.
Geoff Rixon

Left: RT981 was one of the many long-lived members of this famous class. It is seen here at Tattenham Corner, working from Reigate garage, on 5 June 1976 on the 406 to Kingston. *Peter Plummer*

Above: The precise prototype of a handsome EFE model, right down to the route, RCL2244 takes it easy in Dorking garage on Sunday 26 February 1978. A housing estate now occupies the site. The RCL lives on in model form. *Geoff Rixon*

Below: A typical Sunday line-up of RTs resting is recorded on 21 June 1964, before taking up local Monday to Saturday duties around Crawley. From left to right are Nos 3653, 771, 1053, 4731 and 4521. There was a time when a lighter shade of green dominated the Crawley scene: Southdown once provided most of the town services. These were transferred to LCBS operation in 1971. *Hugh Ramsey*

Right: Crawley bus station is pictured on 31 January 1981. Leyland Atlantean AN201, bearing C Line identification and operating on route C2 towards Langley Green, overtakes AEC Reliance RP16 on the Green Line route 750. The 90 members of the RP class were delivered in 1971 and 1972 and largely eliminated RMC and RCL double-deck vehicles from Green Line routes. All were fitted with internal luggage racks and the first 30, of which RP16 was one, were also fitted with boots at the rear for use on touring and private hire work. The C Line reorganisation occurred on 1 July 1978 when the existing pattern of local services in the town was recast; the new services were initially allocated AN double-deck buses and operated with a 20p flat fare. The fleet livery was further embellished on the allocated vehicles with the slogan 'C Line — Crawley's own bus service'. *Geoff Rixon*

Left: RT4747, one of the 1954 deliveries (and stored until 1958) is captured at Sandcross Lane, Reigate, with an isolated double-deck working on the 430 route. At this time, 1973, the route was largely in the hands of AEC Merlins. *Roy Hobbs*

Below: Another of the early batch of AEC Reliances, RP4, stands on the forecourt of Reigate garage about to set off on the rail-air service from Gatwick to Reading on 3 January 1981. *Geoff Rixon*

Left: A positively gleaming Central Area RF423 — note the Mill Hill advert — on loan to Reigate garage loads up at Reigate Red Cross in October 1965.
Roy Hobbs

Below left: Reigate garage, headquarters of the Country Area in London Transport days, is the location for this wonderful collection of what might well be considered the all-time classic double- and single-deck buses — red and green RTs and RFs — with, in the shadows behind the red RF (RF316), a GS. The date is September 1967.
Roy Hobbs

Right: A lady peers carefully around Leatherhead's RT4202, which has almost completed its run from Kingston to Redhill station outside Reigate garage on route 406, before crossing the road in March 1973.
Roy Hobbs

47

Left: Crews, in animated conversation, stand alongside RMC1477, which had recently acquired National green, outside Reigate garage during the summer of 1978. *Roy Hobbs*

Below: RMC1461 swings off the A25 in Reigate town centre and heads towards the North Downs and outer suburbia in September 1978. Although the paintwork is shiny enough, the front dome is rather battered and 'via Epsom Road' hardly encompasses all the places the Routemaster will pass through on its way to its ultimate destination. *Roy Hobbs*

Above: Bournemouth Corporation No 192, a 1965 Daimler Fleetline with Weymann bodywork, is seen at West Croydon on 6 January 1976 whilst running over route 470 to Dorking. *R. C. Riley*

Right: Godstone's almost new RML2307, although covered with a liberal sprinkling of dust, is pictured at the Hardwicke Road terminus of the 411 during the spring of 1966. This series of RMLs were the first Routemaster buses, as opposed to coaches, to enter Country Area service, arriving in the latter part of 1965. The majority eventually found their way back to London Transport ownership and many are still at work in central London. A handful of red RMLs were loaned to London Country for a few weeks pending delivery of its own vehicles. *Roy Hobbs*

Left: Whatever one thinks of the standard National Bus Company livery, it has to be said that brand-new Park Royal-bodied Atlantean AN175, on its first day in service on the 411, makes a splendid sight. It is seen at the summit of Grammar School Hill, Reigate, in October 1978. *Roy Hobbs*

Below: London's first rear-engined double-deck buses, in the shape of 50 Leyland Atlanteans and eight Daimler Fleetlines, all with provincial Park Royal 72-seat bodies, were delivered in 1965. They operated in comparison with the RML class in both the Central and Country areas.

In terms of comfort, appearance and reliability the half-cab won hands down. There have been few less prepossessing-looking buses in the postwar years than the XAs and XFs; internally they were crude and the Atlanteans in particular were unreliable. The Atlanteans were all banished to Hong Kong in 1973, but the Fleetline chassis was chosen as London Transport's standard for the new generation of one-person double-deck vehicles. Six XAs were sent to East Grinstead garage in the spring of 1966 to work the 424 route. XA5 is seen heading for Reigate station, whilst RF591 loads up on the opposite side of the road in late 1967. *Roy Hobbs*

Left: This is the scene inside East Grinstead garage on 7 August 1976. RT4742, drafted in to help out ailing Routemasters, for which spare parts were proving a terrible headache at this time, stands alongside XF4 and a preserved Central Area RT. *R. C. Riley*

Right: The last original London Country Fleetline in service, XF3, is caught on the Surrey/Sussex border on 12 February 1981 shortly before withdrawal on route 438 to Crawley. By this date it was the last former London Transport bus still in normal London Country service. It has been preserved along with XF1. Earlier in its career, XF3 was fitted with a non-standard Cummins V6-200 engine from 1966 until 1973 when the standard Gardner 6LX was restored. *Geoff Rixon*

Above: The Surrey countryside in the morning of early summer sees MB87, one of London Country's earliest Merlins (delivered in 1968), south of Reigate as the bus negotiates the narrow country lanes with a Redhill-bound service on route 425. *Roy Hobbs*

Right: A total of 11 Northern Counties-bodied Daimler Fleetlines was diverted from Western Welsh to London Country in 1972. These vehicles were designated AF by London Country and were allocated to the 410 route from Godstone garage. The penultimate member of the batch, AF10, is recorded at Bromley North on 2 July 1976. *R. C. Riley*

57

Above: Daimler Fleetline CRL6 AF2 is pictured west of Oxted on its way from Bromley to Reigate in April 1978. Intended for the 410, the AFs sometimes appeared on the 409 and 411. All were withdrawn after a short life of eight years. *Geoff Rixon*

Right: One of the Massey-bodied Leyland Atlanteans which Maidstone Borough Council hired out to London Country in 1977 stands at the 410 terminus in Bromley ready to depart with passengers for the Biggin Hill air show on 15 June 1977. *Peter Plummer*

Left: In order to alleviate one of its periodic vehicle shortages, LCBS acquired three ex-Southdown Leyland PD3s in 1975. One of the trio, LS3, is pictured in Godstone, to which garage it was allocated, whilst operating on the 409 route to Forest Row in late 1975. The PD3s were replaced by Leyland Atlanteans on the route during July 1977 and subsequently put up for sale. *D. T. Elliott*

Below: A Maidstone Borough Council Massey-bodied Leyland Atlantean, hired to help out on the 403 as a result of vehicle shortages, stands beside RCL2246, still in Lincoln green, and RMC1474, in National green, at Chelsham on 9 September 1977. *R. C. Riley*

Left: Double-deck vehicles of two generations stand in the autumnal sun at Chelsham on 9 September 1977. On the left is RT1058, nominally on the 403, whilst on the right is RCL2221 on the 453. *R. C. Riley*

Below: Also pictured at Chelsham, but this time on 25 May 1976, another RT, No 604, is seen alongside T2. The single-deck vehicle was one of a quartet of AEC Reliances with Harrington Wayfarer coach bodies bought by LCBS as trainers from Maidstone & District in 1974. The vehicles were new in 1961. *R. C. Riley*

As part of NBC, Green Line coaches ventured far beyond their
traditional Home Counties confines. TD2, a Duple-bodied Leyland
Tiger, takes on seaside-bound passengers at Thamesmead on 16 August
1983. *Peter Plummer*

Pictured at Sevenoaks on 9 August 1974 are two of the earlier Bristol LHSs with ECW bodywork. In the foreground is BL1, on the 404 route, whilst behind is sister vehicle BL4, which is on route 421. BL1 carries a DG (Dunton Green) plate. The vehicles of the BL class were 8ft wide; another batch of Bristol LHSs, the BN class, were only 7ft 6in in width. The 67 vehicles acquired were not destined to have a long career with London Country, being withdrawn and sold after less than a decade of use. *R. C. Riley*

Left: Although relegated to duties as the Northfleet (NF) trainer, RT1102 looks in reasonable external condition as it stands awaiting its next duty at Sevenoaks on 19 February 1975. A total of some 484 RTs passed to London Country ownership on 1 January 1970, but the numbers were quickly reduced. By mid-February 1973 only some 114 remained, many of which were allocated to driver training. *R. C. Riley*

Below: Photographed at Northfleet in early 1976 is one of the ex-Ribble Leyland PD3s with Burlingham bodies acquired by London Country for training purposes in 1975. Originally numbered 1511 by Ribble, LR11 was new in 1957 and has been repainted in London Country's all-yellow livery for training buses. *D. T. Elliott*

Below: With RTs and RFs being life-expired, Routemasters falling by the wayside for lack of spares and their replacements proving far from reliable, London Country was in desperate straits in the late 1970s. Amongst the more unlikely stopgaps were some ex-Royal Blue ECW-bodied Bristol MW6G coaches. No 1425, allocated to Dunton Green, stands in Sevenoaks bus station, with the rear of a Maidstone & District Fleetline just visible in the background, on 23 August 1977. *Peter Plummer*

Right: RCL2241 demonstrates just how dirty it was possible for a London Country bus to get at Greenhithe on 11 February 1978. *Peter Plummer*

Above: SMA6 speeds through Beckenham on 13 July 1976. There were 21 of these distinctive-looking buses. The SMA class were AEC Swifts with Alexander 45-seat bodies that had been intended for South Wales Transport but were diverted when new in 1972 and made their home on route 725. *R. C. Riley*

Right: Despite being over 25 years old, RF202 was still considered fit for Green Line service. It is seen here at Harmer Street, Gravesend, on 30 October 1977. It was to prove the very last RF in either London Country or London Transport service, being eventually withdrawn in July 1979. Not surprisingly it has been preserved, although without its original registration. *Peter Plummer*

Left: RCL2226, pictured in Lincoln green livery, is seen on its way to Brands Hatch on special Green Line route 719 at Swanley on 18 July 1976. *Peter Plummer*

Above: RF221 is recorded with an uninformative blind at Foots Cray on 28 October 1977. The original route 492, from Gravesend to Northumberland Bottom, was one of those inherited by the London Passenger Transport Board from Maidstone & District in the Gravesend area on 1 July 1933. *Peter Plummer*

Left: Another of the fleets that supplied buses to London Country during the dark days of the 1970s was Eastbourne Corporation. Here, one of the municipal operator's AEC Regent Vs with East Lancs rear-entrance bodywork is pictured at Orpington on 3 April 1976, working on the 477 route to Chelsfield. *R. C. Riley*

Above: A seemingly well-maintained RCL2240 of Grays — a garage which at that time was host to many withdrawn London Country Routemasters — is pictured at Tilbury Riverside on 26 February 1977. Sold to London Transport in 1978, RCL2240 is still in service as an open-topper with Arriva and is currently based at Wandsworth garage. *Peter Plummer*

Left: Another Grays Routemaster, RCL2252, is captured at Stifford Clays on 16 May 1978. I met up with this vehicle 20 years later on the other side of the Atlantic in the rather more spectacular setting of Niagara Falls, where the bus now operates sightseeing trips on the Canadian side of the Falls. *Peter Plummer*

Above: Introduced in 1965, the RC class of AEC Reliances with Willowbrook bodywork proved to be something of a failure, although they inaugurated new standards of seating and comfort. They first appeared in a new livery of flake grey and green, but this was altered to standard Green Line livery during 1968. By the early 1970s, the vehicles were largely associated with the 723 route. Here RC10 is pictured at Aldgate in the late spring of 1974. *R. C. Riley*

Left: In August 1973, RF246 is recorded at Victoria whilst operating over the 708 route towards Hemel Hempstead. *R. C. Riley*

Right: If only the roads around Whitehall were always this quiet... On 4 October 1972, London Country RT3255 heads through the Central Area whilst undertaking driver training duties. *R. C. Riley*

Index of Locations

Front cover: Caught in the sun at St Albans on 10 June 1975, Leyland National SNB103 is seen on the 313 route. This route linked St Albans with Enfield and ran via London Colney, South Mimms and Potters Bar. The 313 route was inherited by London General Country Services from the National Omnibus & Transport Co Ltd in March 1932 prior to the LPTB take-over in 1933. Behind the National is AEC Merlin MBS300 on route 354 to Marshalswick. *R. C. Riley*

Back cover: A duo of RMCs — Nos 1511 and 1515 — along with a quartet of RCLs — Nos 2228, 2238, 2234 and 2256 — bask in the sun at Chelsham in September 1978. *Roy Hobbs*